Searchlight BOOKS

World Traveler

D1708852

Travel to

Israel

Matt Doeden

Lerner Publications ◆ Minneapolis

Content consultant: Joni Sussman, publisher, Kar-Ben Publishing; past president, Jewish Community Relations Council of Minnesota and the Dakotas

Lerner Publications Company
An imprint of Lerner Publishing Group, Inc.
241 First Avenue North
Minneapolis, MN 55401 USA

For reading levels and more information, look up this title at www.lernerbooks.com.

Main body text set in Adrianna Regular.
Typeface provided by Chank.

Designer: Mary Ross

Library of Congress Cataloging-in-Publication Data

Names: Doeden, Matt, author.
Title: Travel to Israel / Matt Doeden.
Description: Minneapolis : Lerner Publications, [2022] | Series: Searchlight books - world traveler | Includes bibliographical references and index. | Audience: Ages 8–11 | Audience: Grades 4–6 | Summary: "People have lived in modern-day Israel for thousands of years, and the land is special to those of many religions. Explore Israel's rich history, famous landmarks, celebrations, and more in this guide to the country"— Provided by publisher.
Identifiers: LCCN 2021022717 (print) | LCCN 2021022718 (ebook) | ISBN 9781728441641 (lib. bdg.) | ISBN 9781728448824 (pbk.) | ISBN 9781728445007 (eb pdf)
Subjects: LCSH: Israel—Juvenile literature.
Classification: LCC DS118 .D64 2022 (print) | LCC DS118 (ebook) | DDC 956.94—dc23

LC record available at https://lccn.loc.gov/2021022717
LC ebook record available at https://lccn.loc.gov/2021022718

Manufactured in the United States of America
1-49919-49762-9/8/2021

Table of Contents

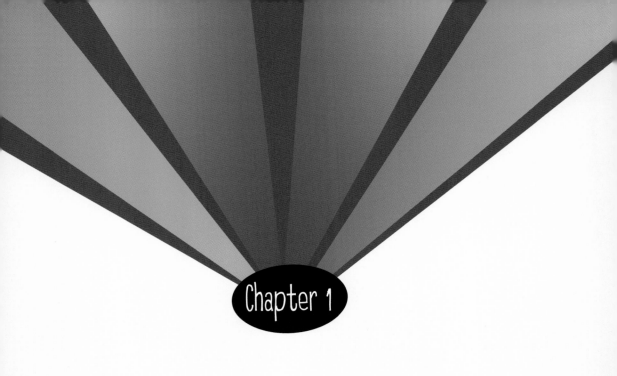

Chapter 1

GEOGRAPHY AND CLIMATE

Israel is a land packed with diversity. Hot deserts, deep valleys, rolling hills, and sandy beaches give this nation its natural beauty.

Israel covers just 8,470 square miles (21,937 sq. km). It's a little bigger than New Jersey and is the 152nd-largest country in the world. Israel shares borders with Egypt, Jordan, Lebanon, and Syria and the territory of Gaza. It controls areas called the Golan Heights and the West Bank.

The Land

Four main regions make up Israel. The coastal plain is a narrow strip of land along the Mediterranean Sea. This flat, fertile land is good for growing fruit and other crops.

The central highlands rise farther inland. At 3,963 feet (1,208 m) above sea level, Mount Meron is Israel's highest

A Mediterranean beach in northern Israel

point. It stands in the region of Galilee near Israel's northern border. The Samarian Hills and the Judean Hills are also part of the central highlands.

The Jordan Rift Valley marks part of Israel's eastern border. This valley cuts deep into the land. In the northern part of Israel, its steep walls track the course of the Jordan River.

The Negev Desert covers most of southern Israel. The land here is rugged and dry. Many parts of the Negev receive only a few inches of rain each year.

A sandstone formation in the Negev Desert

Must-See Stop:
Ein Gedi Nature Reserve

Ein Gedi Nature Reserve is a bright patch of green in the desert. Natural springs give water to the area, allowing plants and animals to thrive. Visitors can spot animals such as wolves, foxes, and ibex. They can visit a waterfall, stroll through the ruins of an ancient village, and see the remains of a temple built more than five thousand years ago.

The Jordan River flows through the Galilee in northern Israel.

Rivers and Lakes

The Jordan is Israel's longest river. It begins in the mountains of Syria, flows into the Sea of Galilee, and ends at the Dead Sea. Other rivers in Israel include the Kishon and the Yarkon.

The Sea of Galilee, or Lake Tiberias, is Israel's largest freshwater lake. It is also the lowest freshwater lake in the world. It lies 696 feet (212 m) below sea level.

To the south lies the Dead Sea. This saltwater lake is about 1,410 feet (430 m) below sea level. The water in the Dead Sea is almost ten times saltier than ocean water. Plants and animals cannot live in such salty water, which explains the sea's name.

Climate

Israel has hot, dry summers and cooler, wetter winters. The coolest places are near the Mediterranean Sea. These places also have more rain than other parts of the country. As you move inland, the weather becomes hotter and drier. Much of the Negev Desert is arid, with very little rainfall.

Palm trees grow well in Israel's hot, dry climate.

Chapter 2

HISTORY AND GOVERNMENT

Israel has existed as a nation only since 1948. But its land has a long, rich history. Scientists have found stone tools of prehistoric people in Israel. The tools were used to cut up plants, animal bones, and meat. Some are more than one hundred thousand years old.

▲

ARCHAEOLOGISTS HAVE FOUND SKULLS AND OTHER PREHISTORIC HUMAN REMAINS IN ISRAEL.

Early Israel

Around 1200 BCE, the Israelite culture emerged in this land. The Israelites developed the Jewish religion. They also created a kingdom, with its capital at Jerusalem. Over the centuries, foreign conquerors took over parts of Israel. They included the Assyrians, Babylonians, and Persians.

The Tower of David in Jerusalem dates to the second century BCE.

Roman armies came to Israel in 63 BCE. The Jews revolted against Roman rule. Eventually Roman armies crushed the rebellion. The Romans expelled Jewish people from Jerusalem. Many left their homeland and scattered throughout the Middle East and Europe.

Israel became part of a land known as Palestine. For many centuries, it was a land of conflict. Muslims and Christians each conquered and controlled the area at times.

A New State

In the late 1800s, European Jews started the Zionist movement. The Zionists wanted Jews to return to Israel to set up a nation in their ancient homeland.

During World War II (1939–1945), the Nazi Party of Germany killed more than six million European Jews. This event, known as the Holocaust, shocked the world. It helped build support for a Jewish nation in Palestine. The United Nations voted for the creation of Israel in 1947. Israel declared its statehood in 1948.

In the 1950s, many Israelis lived on communal farms called kibbutzim.

Many Jews were already living in Israel. Once Israel became a country, Jewish people from all around the globe flocked to live in the land of their ancestors.

A Troubled Beginning

Israelis set about building their new nation. But the creation of Israel angered Arab people already living in Palestine.

In 1948 five Arab nations invaded Israel. Israel won this War of Independence.

David Ben-Gurion (*center*), Israel's first prime minister, celebrates Israeli statehood in 1948.

Let's Celebrate:
Yom Ha'atzmaut

Yom Ha'atzmaut, celebrated in March or April each year, marks Israel's founding in 1948. People gather for speeches, parades, and musical performances. They throw parties, light fireworks, and enjoy foods such as hummus and chocolate cookie truffles. Many wrap up the holiday by singing and dancing.

A meeting of the
Israeli Knesset

Government

Israel is a democracy. Citizens elect leaders to hold
government offices.

The national government is split into three branches.
The legislature—the Knesset—makes the nation's laws.
The executive branch carries out the laws. The prime
minister leads the executive branch. The judicial branch
is made up of courts and judges. They ensure laws are
carried out fairly. The Supreme Court is the highest court
in Israel.

CULTURE AND PEOPLE

About 74 percent of Israel's people are of Jewish descent. About three-quarters of these people were born in Israel. The remaining one-quarter came to Israel from other places, such as Russia, Latin America, and other parts of the Middle East. Arab people make up about 21 percent of the population. People from a variety of other ethnic backgrounds make up the remaining 5 percent.

Religion

Judaism is the official religion of Israel. One of the world's oldest religions, Judaism grew out of early Israelite traditions. Jews believe in one God. The teachings of Judaism are written down in the Hebrew Bible and other sacred texts.

Jewish men pray at the Western Wall in Jerusalem.

About 18 percent of Israel's people are Muslims. They follow the Islamic religion. This faith was founded in the 600s CE on the Arabian Peninsula.

About 2 percent of Israel's people are Christians. Other religious groups, including the Druze, make up the rest of Israel's population.

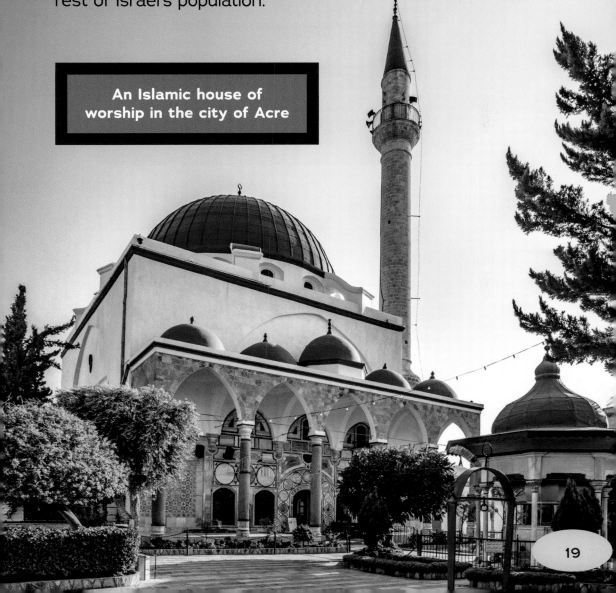

An Islamic house of worship in the city of Acre

Many Israeli road signs are written in (*from top to bottom*) Hebrew, Arabic, and English.

Language and Writing

Hebrew was the language of the ancient Israelites. The spoken language died out around 200 CE, after Roman armies drove the Jews from Jerusalem. The language was revived in the late 1800s. In 1948 it became the official language of Israel.

Hebrew writing uses an alphabet of twenty-two characters. When people write in Hebrew, they start on the right side of the page. The words move from right to left—the opposite of English writing.

Arabic is also an official language of Israel. Many of Israel's people speak English or Russian as well.

Food and Art

Israel's food is a unique blend of Jewish and Arab traditions. Chickpeas are a staple of Israeli cuisine. They can be mashed up to make hummus or mashed and deep-fried to make falafel. Israel's people also enjoy locally grown produce, such as dates and lemons.

Israel's people come from all over and have brought many artistic styles to Israel. Traditional Israeli paintings often show natural scenes or Jewish religious figures. Some artists make ornate jewelry out of silver.

Some Israeli performers tell the history of their people through folk songs and dance. The Israel Philharmonic Orchestra is world famous.

A boy watches a street vendor prepare falafel in Jerusalem.

Must-See Stop:
The Dead Sea

The Dead Sea is one of Israel's natural wonders. It is a popular tourist stop. The large amounts of salt in the sea make the water very dense, or heavy. Our bodies are lighter than the water, so it is easy for people to float on the surface. But they need to take care when they swim in the sea. The salt crystals in the water can sting swimmers' eyes and even cut their skin.

Chapter 4

DAILY LIFE

Modern Israel is home to more than nine million people. It is the ninety-seventh most populated country in the world. Most of Israel's people live in urban areas. Jerusalem is the capital, with more than eight hundred thousand residents. Tel Aviv is Israel's largest metropolitan area. Haifa and Ashdod are other large cities.

Education is important in Israel. All children attend school through twelfth grade. When they are young adults, most Jewish Israelis serve in the nation's military for several years.

Israel has a strong economy. It is home to many computer technology businesses. Many solar power businesses are also based in Israel.

ISRAEL'S ASHALIM POWER STATION PRODUCES SOLAR POWER.

Let's Celebrate:
Tu B'Shevat

A connection to nature is important to Israel's people. In January or February of each year, they celebrate that connection with Tu B'Shevat. The holiday dates back to the ancient Israelites. In modern times, Israelis celebrate Tu B'Shevat by planting trees.

Future Challenges

Israel faces many challenges. The Palestinian conflict is one of the most pressing. World leaders have tried many times to bring peace to Israel. But conflict continues in the 2020s.

Tel Aviv is a bustling, modern city.

Researchers study cells at an Israeli biotechnology company.

Another problem for Israel is its rapid growth. Its population is booming. But Israel is a small nation with limited natural resources. As the population grows, Israel must figure out how to provide people with enough clean water and healthy food.

Israel's growth also has many benefits. In less than eighty years, Israel grew from a brand-new nation into an economic superpower. Israelis hope their country will continue to prosper and will also become more peaceful.

Map and Key Facts

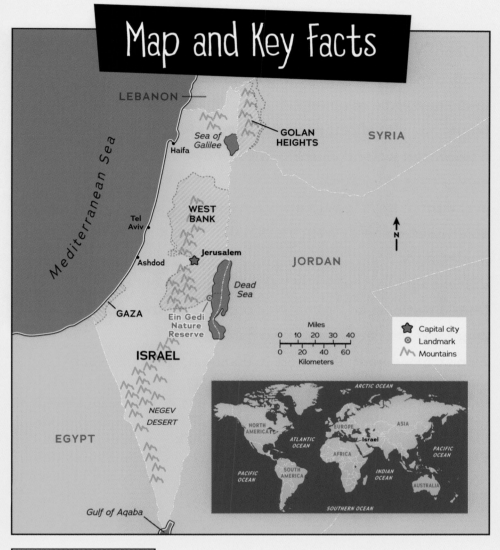

Flag of Israel

- Continent: Asia
- Capital city: Jerusalem
- Population: 9 million
- Languages: Hebrew, Arabic, Russian, and English

Glossary

Arab: a member of a large Middle Eastern ethnic group

arid: having little or no rainfall

falafel: spicy fried patties made of ground-up chickpeas

freshwater: water containing little or no salt

ibex: a type of wild goat

prehistoric: existing before written history

solar power: energy from the sun that is used to create heat or electricity

statehood: the condition of being an independent nation

United Nations: an international organization that works for peace and the betterment of humankind

Zionist movement: the effort to establish a national homeland for the Jewish people in Israel

Learn More

Dead Sea Facts for Kids
   https://kids.kiddle.co/Dead_Sea

Israel: Land of Creation
   https://israel.travel

National Geographic Kids: Israel
   https://kids.nationalgeographic.com/geography/countries/article
   /israel

Ofanansky, Allison. *Tisha B'Av: A Jerusalem Journey*. Minneapolis: Kar-Ben,
   2017.

Rechner, Amy. *Israel*. Minneapolis: Bellwether Media, 2018.

Spanier, Kristine. *Israel*. Minneapolis: Pogo Books, 2020.

Index

Photo Acknowledgments

Image credits: Sharon Duak Pikiwiki Israel/Wikimedia Commons (CC BY 2.5), p. 5; Miroslav Orincak/Shutterstock.com, p. 6; vvvita/Shutterstock.com, p. 7; Giovanni G/Shutterstock.com, p. 8; Sergei25/Shutterstock.com, p. 9; ChameleonsEye/Shutterstock.com, pp. 11, 20; Seth Aronstam/Shutterstock.com, p. 12; Kibbutz Beit Zera Archive/Wikimedia Commons (CC BY-SA 4.0), p. 13; AFP/Getty Images, p. 14; chameleonseye/iStock/Getty Images, pp. 15, 25; Itzik Edri PikiWiki Israel/Wikimedia Commons (CC BY 2.5), p. 16; Yadid Levy/Shutterstock.com, p. 18; trabantos/Shutterstock.com, p. 19; Saeed Qaq/APA Images/ZUMA Press, Inc./Alamy Stock Photo, p. 21; NDStock/iStock/Getty Images, p. 22; Photographer Lili/Shutterstock.com, p. 24; Dmitry Pistrov/Shutterstock.com, pp. 26–27; Eddie Gerald/Alamy Stock Photo, p. 28; Laura K. Westlund, p. 29.

Cover: Photographer Lili/Shutterstock.com.